STUDIES IN ENGLISH LITERATURE No. 38

General Editor

David Daiches

Professor of English in the School of English and
American Studies, University of Sussex

To
K. F. M.

SWIFT:
GULLIVER'S TRAVELS

by

ANGUS ROSS

*Reader in English in the School of English and
American Studies, University of Sussex*

EDWARD ARNOLD

First published 1968 by
Edward Arnold (Publishers) Ltd.,
41 Maddox Street, London W1

Cloth edition SBN: 7131 5448 9

Paper edition SBN: 7131 5449 7

Printed in Great Britain by
The Camelot Press Ltd., London and Southampton

General Preface

It has become increasingly clear in recent years that what both the advanced sixth-former and the university student need most by way of help in their literary studies are close critical analyses and evaluations of individual works. Generalisations about periods or authors, general chat about the Augustan Age or the Romantic Movement, have their uses; but all too often they provide merely the illusion of knowledge and understanding of literature. All too often students come up to the university under the impression that what is required of them in their English Literature courses is the referring of particular works to the appropriate generalisations about the writer or his period. Without taking up the anti-historical position of some of the American 'New Critics', we can nevertheless recognise the need for critical studies that concentrate on the work of literary art rather than on its historical background or cultural environment.

The present series is therefore designed to provide studies of individual plays, novels and groups of poems and essays, which are known to be widely studied in sixth forms and in universities. The emphasis is on clarification and evaluation; biographical and historical facts, while they may of course be referred to as helpful to an understanding of particular elements in a writer's work, will be subordinated to critical discussion. What kind of work is this? What exactly goes on here? How good is this work, and why? These are the questions which each writer will try to answer.

DAVID DAICHES

Contents

si donc les livres du Sieur Gulliver ne sont calcules que pour les Isles Britannique, ce voyageur doit passer pour un tres pitoyable Ecrivain. les memes vices, et les memes follies regnent par tout, du moins, dans les pays civilises de l'Europe, et l'auteur qui n'ecrit que pour une ville, une province, un Royaume, ou meme un siecle, merite si peu d'etre traduit qu'il ne merite pas d'etre lu.

Swift's draft of a letter to
l'Abbé des Fontaines, July, 1727

Introduction

Two qualities are common to all Swift's greatest works, however different they may be in kind: these are strenuous energy and concise expression. These are also two of the most valuable weapons of the satirist, with which he knocks the settled views of the complacent reader off balance. Swift, however, employs them with a strength and agility which taxes the reader's dodging ability to the utmost, and this makes him in some respects the most disturbing writer in the English language. Readers have responded to his bewildering force in several ways. They have ignored what they could not accept. They have tried to explain parts of his writings as meaning not what they seem to mean, but what they ought to mean in order to fit into a harmonious, and therefore calmer and less disturbing, scheme. The elements of spontaneity and opportunism that exist in the texture of Swift's works are in this way often ignored or seen as something unacceptable, instead of another facet of the strange life that exists in his writing. Historians of ideas have sought to bring order out of apparently contradictory arguments and attitudes by documenting Swift's education, the antecedents of his intellectual positions, and the contemporary background of his diverse beliefs, feelings and prejudices. Biographers have attempted to show an inner or hidden consistency in Swift's life (psychological theorising has proved useful here), which in turn would allow a pattern to be imposed on the works themselves; and it is of course true that Swift's life is a fascinating study, and in his letters, for example, he has left documents of moving human value which have puzzled many. Historians of literature can produce antecedents for the different kinds of books he writes and a scheme for his principles of literary judgement; this also allows a more rational choice to the reader among the rapid shifts and succession of ideas, impressions and feelings which rise up from Swift's text. Critics have analysed individual works and passages, and by a study of rhetorical structure or satirical techniques have attempted to establish a controlling artistic aim which could form a pattern easily accessible to the reader. All these approaches have their value, and have given rise to some brilliant and subtle studies. Any writer on Swift is immediately placed in the debt of many forerunners, and this debt will obviously be marked in the present brief discussion of Gulliver's *Travels*, though no footnotes have been provided to indicate particular borrowings. It is hoped a general statement will be sufficient. The stability which many of the studies of Swift have sought to produce, however, is precarious, and while together they provide excellent help, a survey of them leads the reader back to his original impression of a variety of patterns in Swift's works, the powerful interaction of sometimes incompatible attitudes, and the resulting unforgettable and very human restlessness which informs the sheer brilliance of the writing. To read a work by Swift is not a passive occupation, but an active affair.

Gulliver's *Travels*, the most widely read of Swift's works, is also the best instance of the difficulty critics and historians have in approaching and discussing the satirist's writing. The benevolent Sir Walter Scott considered that 'we are compelled to admire the force of his talents, even while thus unworthily employed, in exposing the worst parts of our nature', the difficulty of course being the *Travels*, that 'libel on human nature'. This is perhaps understandable, but a work is worth closer examination that can provoke Thackeray, himself a satirist though no admirer of Swift's own age, to his famous hysterical outburst about the *Travels* as: 'horrible, shameful, unmanly, blasphemous; and giant and great as this Dean is, I say we should hoot him', adding that no one should read Book IV, the work of a 'monster gibbering shrieks and gnashing imprecatious against mankind,—tearing down all shreds of modesty, past all sense of manliness and shame; filthy in word, filthy in thought, furious, raging, obscene.' Somewhat later, Sir Edmund Gosse lamented that the horrible foulness of the last voyage 'banishes from decent households a fourth part of one of the most brilliant and delightful of English books.' One of the commonplaces of the criticism of this book is the irony that lies in the process by which a careful, profound and 'gloomy' satire, the work of a savage wit, has become a children's book. For many years, all during the nineteenth century and in some cases still, it is the editors (and critics) who have made Swift's work into a children's story, by simply omitting passages that wouldn't fit into a simple narrative pattern. There doesn't seem anything very ironical about insensitive editors making the book into a children's story, along (probably quite wrong) lines which they think will interest the young.

This is only one form of expurgation. The Oxford Clarendon Press edition of Gulliver's *Travels* by A. B. Gough omitted passages which the editor thought scatalogical and 'unnecessary' for Swift's purposes: but then the book was made to conform to Gough's idea of Swift's purposes.

Swift's wit is constantly at work and his irony pervasive, so that any omissions damage the total impact.

The truth is that the book has many 'levels' of meaning, and one of them certainly is the kind of imagination and fancy in which children's tales abound. Swift has the ability to create a world, or worlds, where ordinary things are different, smaller, larger, or topsy-turvy. This is not a simpler, less important level of the work which can be ignored in favour of more subtle or profound levels, but something which must be considered (and is certainly felt) along with these other 'levels'. It defines them, or conflicts with them, or affects them in some way. Equally, however, it is not to be presented as the only content.

In fact much of the confusion in dealing with Gulliver's *Travels* comes from the desire to pin down *one* 'meaning' in the book, *one* moral, *one* conclusion. Sometimes this simplistic version is seen in autobiographical terms: is Swift a pessimist? a misogynist? a misanthrope? a Christian priest? a psychotic with an anal fixation? and so on. These questions are beside the mark. A pluralist way of taking the book allows the reader access to several 'meanings' which it has. Like everyone else, Swift was by turns a good number of characters, and while a single view of his character may be of interest and value in elucidating problems in his writings, it cannot be a controlling principle in dealing with a work.

One difficulty is, of course, that Swift uses a variety of satirical methods. This procedure allows many possibilities in 'meaning' to exist at any one time, and cannot be responded to in terms of some monolithic, single content. Each of the four voyages works differently. For example, on each one, Gulliver gets new clothes. Compare the four passages:

Two hundred Sempstresses were employed to make me Shirts. . . . The Sempstresses took my Measure as I lay on the Ground, one standing at my Neck, and another at my Mid-Leg, with a strong Cord extended, that each held by the End, while the third measured the Length of the Cord with a Rule of an Inch long. Then they measured my right Thumb, and desired no more; for by a mathematical Computation, that twice round the Thumb is once round the Wrist, and so on to the Neck and the Waist; and by the Help of my old Shirt, which I displayed on the Ground before them for a pattern, they fitted me exactly. . . .

Book I

The Queen likewise ordered the thinnest Silks that could be gotten, to make me Cloaths; not much thicker than an *English* blanket, very cumbersome till I was accustomed to them. They were after the Fashion of the Kingdom, partly resembling the *Persian*, and partly the Chinese; and are a very grave decent habit.

Book II

... the King ... ordered a Taylor to come next Morning, and take my Measure for a suit of Cloths. This Operator did his Office after a different Manner from those of his Trade in *Europe*. He first took my Altitude by a Quadrant, and then with a Rule and Compasses, described the Dimensions and Out-Lines of my whole Body; all which he entred upon Paper, and in six Days, brought my Cloths very ill made, and quite out of Shape, by happening to mistake a Figure in the Calculation.

Book III

When my Cloaths were worn to Rags, I made my self others with the Skins of Rabbets, and of a certain beautiful Animal about the same Size, called the *Nnuhnoh*, the Skin of which is covered with a fine Down. Of these I likewise made very tolerable Stockings. I soaled my Shoes with Wood which I cut from a Tree, and fitted to the upper Leather, and when this was worn out, I supplied it with the Skins of Yahoos, dried in the Sun.

Book IV

In the first passage from the 'Voyage to Lilliput' the emphasis is witty. Gulliver is amused, and is given a minute, rather condescending (half-admiring) report to transmit to the readers. The working out of the size difference provides a joke, and the ingenuity of the Lilliputians is stressed. The clothes passage is not really a local satirical area in the writing, except that if the 'old Shirt' is available as a pattern, the calculations are perhaps hardly needed. In Book II, a 'moral' Book, there is a difference. Gulliver has become a court pet, his clothes are 'ordered', like bones or bird-seed, by the Queen; the size difference is present, but is not worked out in this particular passage. There is, however, a kind of symbolic pointer in the last sentence. The Persians and the Chinese were traditionally sages in European literature, as can be seen in Montesquieu's *Letters Persanes* (1721) and Goldsmith's 'Chinese Letters' (*Citizen of the World*, 1762), and were used by satirists to belabour European pretensions. In Book III, the theme of human ingenuity is taken up again, though the Laputans' abilities are grossly misdirected. Beneath the expected ingenuity of the obvious conceit can be seen lurking either a caricature of Newton as an astronomical tailor, or of the Newtonian picture of God as a kind of mechanic. The satirist implies that Newton is underestimating the complexity of the universe, either by presenting a wrong and simplified picture of God, considering him in a human image, or by presenting a simplified picture of the universe, considering it in terms of the human artefact, or both. Swift underlines the arrogance of Newton's home-made design by ironically referring to the 'six Days', the space of time assigned to the Creation in the biblical account. By relying on unaided human reason, Newton naturally produces a 'very ill-made' creation.

The passage from Book IV is different again. This time Gulliver makes his own clothes. The point of view of the narrator himself is introduced as the topic of careful irony. Book IV is an animal book, where Gulliver's animality is part of the discussion, so in this passage the clothes are con-structed of skins, not man-made textiles. It will be obvious that the reader must treat each of these passages differently. The satirical method is not the same in each. The only thing consistent is Swift's constantly active wit.

Even in a single Book there are differences in texture between passages. In Book II, the second paragraph is a famous parody of a seaman's spate of technical terms which he might throw down on the page to blind the reader with science: it is in fact taken almost verbatim from Samuel Sturmy's *Mariner's Magazine* of 1669. The satirical point is partly the rather modish intention of raillery against excessively technical writing. A later passage describing the king, with a similar, breathless list of nouns, however, is an ancient form of witty satirical writing of a quite different kind:

> HE was perfectly astonished with the historical Account I gave him of our Affairs during the last Century; protesting it was only a Heap of Conspiracies, Rebellions, Murders, Massacres, Revolutions, Banish-ments; the very worst Effects that Avarice, Faction, Hypocrisy, Perfidiousness, Cruelty, Rage, Madness, Hatred, Envy, Lust, Malice, and Ambition could produce.

Here the voice of the satirist himself usurps the place of any of the dramatic interlocutors within the framework. Readers in Swift's own day responded flexibly to this variety of tone. They didn't think every-thing said, for example, was said by Swift. One of his friends, Dr. Arbuthnot, who certainly yields nothing to Thackeray in experience, respectability or humanity, found Gulliver's *Travels* 'such a Merry Book'.

1. Writing and Printing

Gulliver's *Travels* and Robinson Crusoe's *Adventures* are two of the few books of the Augustan age of English Literature that are read by everybody, including people not particularly interested in a close study of the early eighteenth century. Interpretations of such books are liable to swing from free-wheeling, popular readings of 'just the words on the page' to panicky academic reactions ot these sometimes wild, but always genuine responses. Comment on Swift's book provides an involved instance of this critical see-saw. Ignorance of the historical and cultural matrix of the *Travels* can, under the influence of the power of Swift's writing, turn into a contempt for such information. This is a particularly dangerous state of affairs in reading Augustan satire, which was always so deeply rooted in contemporary society. Equally, however, academic definition of what is happening in Swift's complex structure can turn into obsessive intrusion of simplistic explanations rising from the history of ideas, the study of literary forms, or other scholarly pastimes.

In a short survey of the circumstances surrounding the writing and printing of Gulliver's *Travels*, it is hoped to show that the book obviously contained from the beginning a spectrum of meanings, and that it is possible to think of at least part of this spectrum as being *put there*, as a spectrum, by Swift himself. Also, the way in which the book was fitted together could not but encourage a diversity of 'content', which Swift's genius uses not only to enrich his satire, but also for his own purposes to bewilder his readers. This is a rhetorical or tonal difficulty, to be dealt with later. It means, however, that Swift's meaning is deliberately intricate and many-sided.[1]

There is some indication that there are 'hints' in Gulliver's *Travels* that go back as far as June 1711, to the time when Swift, in London, was a member of the political and literary group known as 'the Society', and more important a key member of the inner group known as the

[1] Any writer on Swift is placed inescapably in the debt of the late Sir Harold Williams. The letters referred to in the following paragraphs may be found, by date, in his *Correspondence of Jonathan Swift* (Oxford 1963–65), and he explores the problems of the publication, with acknowledgement to Teerink and other scholars, in *The Text of Gulliver's Travels* (Cambridge 1952).

'Scriblerus Club' which has evolved from the Society by late 1713. This smaller group, containing Dr. Arbuthnot, Pope, Gay, Parnell, as well as Robert Harley, Earl of Oxford and Lord Treasurer, was more interested in wit and writing than in practical politics for their own sake. Naturally, though, the political interests of these Tory gatherings, close to the heart of the government and often containing the Queen's chief minister himself, could not but penetrate all their literary schemes. Obviously then, if a few of Swift's ideas date from this time, they already have a strong political flavour. The Scriblerians were interested in satirising 'false tastes in Learning'. Some of their joint writing shows a high degree of technical, philosophical skill in, for example, sending up in a friendly way some of the notions of George Berkeley, the idealist philosopher. While no doubt Swift entered into this, his purposes are rather different. Pope published the co-operative effort of the club, *The Memoirs of Scriblerus*, in 1727 in the *Miscellanies*, and later on its own in 1741. There are strong parallels between chapter XVI of this work, containing '. . . some hints of [Scriblerus's] Travels', and Gulliver's voyages; also the projects of the Academy of Lagado are echoed in the *Memoirs of Scriblerus*. It is, however, more likely that Pope was using Gulliver's *Travels*, than that Swift was recollecting his work for the *Memoirs*, and most likely that Pope is exaggerating the Scriblerian side of Swift's work. This apparently dry piece of literary history has its importance. Book III of the *Travels* is often thought to be the least successful part of the satire, and this is true if it is thought of as a Scriblerian satire on the false tastes in learning. Such a judgement treats the Book solely, or mainly, from the point of view of the history of ideas, as a witty passage of arms in the ancients and moderns controversy. As usual, however, this is too schematic a way to treat Swift's satire which is not solely a 'document' in the history of ideas. The judgement is not true if there are additional and crucially important meanings in the way the projects and projectors are handled. Then the social and political content of Book III is seen to be integral to the movement of the book, not clumsily grafted on to an intellectual game.

On August 24, 1714, immediately after the death of Queen Anne, Swift retired from London to his deanery in Dublin, and for the next six years there is little known about his intellectual life in what he considered a cruel exile. He published little or nothing, and his letters are uncommunicative. On April 15, 1721, however, he wrote to his friend Charles Ford:

I am now writing a History of my Travells, which will be a large Volume, and give an Account of Countreys hitherto unknown; but they go on slowly for want of Health and Humor.

He was therefore, a fact well known to his friends, putting together the book now known as Gulliver's *Travels*, and for the next few years they keep referring in their letters to the progress of this work. Thus, on January 1, 1722, Bolingbroke wrote to him:

I long to see your Travels.

'Putting together' the book is the best way to think of the process, since it is known that the order in which Swift wrote the 'Travels' is not the same as the order in which they are found in the book. In other words the book will have a pattern, probably, rather than a narrative 'outcome'. On January 19, 1724, we wrote to Ford:

I have left the Country of the Horses, and am in the flying Island, where I shall not stay long and my two last Journeyes will be soon over.

By August 14, 1725, he was able to write to the same correspondent,

I have finished my Travells, and I am now transcribing them; they are admirable Things and will wonderfully mend the World. Meliorist?

Six weeks later he wrote to Pope, on September 29, 1725,

I have employed my Time (besides ditching) in finishing, correcting, amending and Transcribing my Travells, in four parts Compleat newly Augmented, and intended for the Press when the World shall deserve them, or rather when a Printer shall be found brave enough to venture his Eares. . . .

The tone of these letters, the defensive irony, is worth noting, as indicating that Swift probably thinks he has written a masterpiece. The passage from the letter to Pope, with its jocular use of a copy-writer's formula from a book advertisement, and the reference to the punishment for seditious libel, shows that Swift from an early stage has a very conscious notion of the presentation and publication of his masterpiece.

To sum up, the gestation of the book may span a total of fourteen or fifteen years, and the active writing of it spanned a period of at least five years, from 1721 to 1725. The political events directly mentioned in the book are chiefly from this latter period. The book was carefully put together in an order different from the order of writing it. Swift was proud of the book; conscious of the importance of the manner of its

B

presentation to the public; and aware of the danger of prosecution for seditious libel.

The elaboration of the presentation is illustrated by the strange events that surround the printing. Swift came to London for his second last visit in early March 1726, and stayed five months. He obviously brought with him a MS. of his *Travels*, but he did not take steps to have it printed until a few days before he returned to Ireland. On August 8 a letter dictated by Swift, but written out by Gay, and signed 'Richard Sympson' who was said to be Gulliver's cousin, was sent to Benjamin Motte, an important printer and publisher. Accompanying the letter were some specimen pages of the MS. of the book probably in another hand, which may have accounted for part of the delay on Swift's part. Motte was directed to return the MS. if he did not wish to publish the book, but if he did, then he was to send a bank bill for £200 within three days, and then the rest of the MS. would be sent to him. He replied on August 11, that he accepted the MS. for publication, but could not raise £200 so quickly; but if the rest of the MS. were sent, he would publish the book immediately and if it succeeded would send £200 within six months. 'Richard Sympson' accepted these terms on August 13, and Swift left London on August 15.

Some of the point of this strange exercise is of course that the book was politically dangerous. The original letter to Motte admitted that it contained passages which were 'a little satirical' and urged Motte to take advice before committing himself to publishing it. It is also clear, however, that Swift liked the mystification, and pushed the idea of a 'frame' for the book, a cousin for the narrator and the notion that passages *might* be dangerous.

The procedure meant that Swift saw no proofs of the book. It was an immediate success and went through three editions in 1726 alone, as well as being serialised in two separate newspapers. In November, however, Swift is complaining in a letter that the text has been mangled, abused, added to and blotted out. Specific corrections of many gross errors of the press, chiefly verbal, were conveyed to Motte in January 1727, and eventually in 1735, Faulkner, a Dublin printer, brought out an edition corrected, most probably, by Swift himself. There is argument about the status of these corrections, but it is important to notice that when substantive, they concern the satire on contemporary personages, politics, law and society. Even Faulkner left out five paragraphs at the end of Book III, chapter 3, as being too dangerous politically.

The printing history, therefore, reinforces some of the points made by a study of the process of writing. The presentation is extremely important. The book contains an important layer of political material, which is the centre of editorial disturbance. The actual printed work should thus be closely examined and in some respects treated tentatively. Swift's mystification is an important rhetorical device, only partly caused by prudential defence against libel proceedings. It may be concluded without doubt that there is a spectrum of meanings in the book, and that Swift is throwing on the reader a burden of active discrimination, and the necessity of exercising caution in interpretation.

Representation
:public, space,

2. The Conduct of the Satire: Diversity

Gulliver's *Travels* is often thought of as a narrative; but, as is common in Swift's writings, there is more than one thing going on at a time. There are really two narratives. Swift's own skill as a story-teller is being brought into play. He has, of course, complete control of the ordering of Gulliver's voyages, of the adventures that befall him, and so on. Here he exploits to the full a talent which he employs on many occasions in other works, that of objectifying ideas, of making concepts powerfully visual. A simple example is his description of the Struldbruggs:

> He told me, that sometimes, although very rarely, a Child happened to be born in a Family with a red circular Spot in the Forehead, directly over the left Eye-brow, which was an infallible Mark that it should never dye. The Spot, as he described it, was about the Compass of a Silver Threepence, but in the Course of Time grew larger, and changed its Colour; for at Twelve Years old it became green, so continued till Five and Twenty, then turned to a deep blue; . . .

In the same way, he is able to penetrate to the hunger of the imagination on the reader's part that is satisfied by fairy tales, by eyes as big as saucers, by the bean-stalk or by Pinocchio's nose growing inexorably longer, like a tree twig. This power, too, is one of the disconcerting strengths of Swift's poetry. In *A Description of a City Shower*, published in the *Tatler* in 1710, the literary, moral, political and social disorder which Swift detects in London is objectified by the details of the aftermath of the shower. At the end of the poem, he moves from a general mention of 'Filths of all Hues and Odours', by way of a geographically detailed journey, to three of the best lines he ever wrote, which achieve their full effect by a concentration of specific concrete objects.

> NOW from all Parts the swelling Kennels flow,
> And bear their Trophies with them, as they go:
> Filths of all Hues and Odours seem to tell
> What Streets they sail'd from, by the Sight and Smell.
> They, as each Torrent drives, with rapid Force
> From *Smithfield*, or St. *Pulchre's* shape their Course;
> And in huge Confluent join at *Snow-Hill* Ridge,
> Fall from the *Conduit* prone to *Holborn-Bridge*.

> Sweepings from Butchers Stalls, Dung, Guts, and Blood,
> Drown'd Puppies, stinking Sprats, all drench'd in Mud,
> Dead Cats, and Turnip-Tops come tumbling down the Flood.

Similarly in *The Progress of Beauty*, one of his greatest moral and philosophical poems, he makes his point of the relative nature of beauty and appearance by visualising the chaos of cosmetics and sweat running together:

> To see her from her Pillow rise
> All reeking in a cloudy Steam,
> Crackt Lips, foul Teeth, and gummy Eyes,
> Poor Strephon, how would he blaspheme! . . .
>
> Three Colours, Black, and Red, and White,
> So graceful in their proper Place,
> Remove them to a different Light
> They form a frightful hideous Face.
>
> For instance; when the Lilly slipps
> Into the Precincts of the Rose,
> And takes Possession of the Lips
> Leaving the Purple to the Nose.

A similar visual and objectifying imagination permeates *Gulliver's Travels*. At the beginning of chapter 6 of 'A Voyage to Lilliput', though Swift ironically makes Gulliver say that he intends 'to leave the Description of this Empire to a particular Treatise', he also makes him follow this remark with a paragraph of close description of the common size of the natives, their 'Geese about the bigness of a Sparrow', ending with an appeal for help to 'The Reader's Imagination'. The whole of chapter 5 of the same 'Voyage'—an account of the 'Extraordinary Stratagem' by which Gulliver captures the Blefuscan fleet—is another example of 'Swift's narrative'. In Book II, there is even more of this kind of narrative —in chapter 1, the meal at the farmer's dinner table, or the fight with the rats on the bed, or in chapter 2, Gulliver's appearance as a freak in a market-town inn. The imagination turns darker, but works in the same way in Book IV, in such episodes as Gulliver's brush with the Yahoos in chapter 1, when he 'escaped pretty well, by sticking close to the Stem of the Tree'.

This 'narrative' of Swift's is ingenious, interesting, sometimes a little opportunistic. Like the visual detail of a fairy story, Swift's objectifying is very disconcerting if it is pondered. It is as if he sometimes gives himself up almost completely to imagining very hard indeed, 'What it would be like if . . .'. This has led some readers to immerse themselves wholly in the events of the book, to read it simply as a series of adventures. On a more exalted level, too, there is ample opportunity here for a use of these events to present a psychological analysis of Swift's obsessive pictures. But both of these approaches to the book are severely controlled by a contradictory and diverging strain inside the 'story'.

This is the second 'narrative', that of Gulliver himself. On the tension between the two narratives hinges a good deal of the difficulty in interpreting the satire, or at least in giving it a unified meaning. It is obvious that one of the levels of meaning in the book is a satire on travel books, and travellers' tales. Swift clearly read widely in this kind of literature and was fascinated by it, for what is satirised powerfully must in a way be strongly attractive. In the 'Letter from Captain Gulliver' which prefaces the 1735 Faulkner edition, as well as introducing 'Cousin Sympson', Gulliver claims 'cousin Dampier' as a relative, and he further rather improbably claims a hand in the publication of Dampier's book of travels, A [New] Voyage round the World. The old captain and buccaneer published this book in 1697, and other books of voyages around the same time. It is significant that Gulliver confines his advice to how to put the Travels 'in Order, and correct the Style'. The satire on travel books draws attention to Gulliver's 'narrative'. Swift ironically makes Gulliver refer to the surface, the style of such reports, but the real intention is to stress the potential importance of these reports as illuminating the nature of man himself. Swift also contrasts the superficiality of the usual travel book with the depth of his own satire. Most travel writers fill their travels full of empty details. They rarely use their stories to present clear judgements, to illustrate the proper study of mankind, which is man. POPE Instead they concentrate on presenting dishonest images of themselves or merely offer the vain entertainment of a seven days' wonder. Gulliver's narrative often illustrates this, but also at the end of 'A Voyage to Brobdingnag', he actually makes this kind of criticism explicitly himself:

> THE Captain was very well satisfied with this plain Relation I had given him; and said, he hoped when we returned to *England*, I would oblige the World by putting it in Paper, and making it publick. My Answer was, that I thought we were already over-stocked with Books of Travel: That nothing could now pass which was not Extraordinary; wherein I doubted, some Authors less consulted Truth than their own Vanity or Interest, or the Diversion of ignorant Readers. That my

Story could contain little besides common Events, without those ornamental Descriptions of strange Plants, Trees, Birds and other Animals; or the barbarous Customs and Idolatry of savage People, with which most Writers abound. However, I thanked him for his good Opinion, and promised to take the Matter into my Thoughts.

Unfortunately, Gulliver confuses 'ornamental Descriptions' with accounts which could be practically useful. The Royal Society in Swift's age, for example, was quite properly interested in 'strange Plants' and other exotic fruits of the earth, from the point of view of using them for the nutritive and economic benefit of man, as well as for speculative and aesthetic motives. A similar practical interest partly underlay the foundation of the botanical garden at Kew by Princess Augusta in 1759, and more obviously prompted the laying out of botanical gardens in the West Indies later in the eighteenth century. When the mutiny on the *Bounty* took place in 1789, poor Captain Bligh was on a voyage to collect bread-fruit tree plants in Otaheite: these plants were to be introduced into the West Indies to give starch for the slaves' diet, and knowledge of them had come to Europe by mariners' reports. The 'barbarous Customs and Idolatory of savage People' should not be dismissed either, but ideally could have a practical, moral interest, which Gulliver in this passage, like the run of travel writers, misses. They present pictures of man in a state of nature and provide useful comparisons with Christian revelation. In fact, mariners were encouraged by the Royal Society to report on the customs and beliefs as well as on foreign flora and fauna, of strange societies. At the end of 'A Voyage to the Country of the Houyhnhnms', however, Gulliver has some realisation of this true end of travellers' tales:

IT is easy for us who travel into remote Countries, which are seldom visited by *Englishmen* or other *Europeans*, to form Descriptions of wonderful Animals both at Sea and Land. Whereas, a Traveller's chief Aim should be to make Men wiser and better, and to improve their Minds by the bad, as well as the good Example of what they deliver concerning foreign Places.

Part of the effect of Swift's satire comes from fitful flashes like this on Gulliver's part, and from the uncertainty from episode to episode of Gulliver's purposes in writing his narrative. So the satire on 'travellers' tales' and the jokes about accuracy have relevance on several levels.

The narrative level is there, but clearly it is not so simple as it looks.

argumentative value

Indeed, Gulliver's *Travels* can only imperfectly be read as any kind of fiction. If in some novels, perhaps most, the imaginative centre is the narrative itself, and other things, characterisation, dialogue, description and so forth, further this end, so in Gulliver's travels, the centre is *argument*. Most of the other things in the book, the 'character' of Gulliver, the objectified description, the startling events, the ingenious narrative may be thought of as furthering that. In this respect, Swift's book is to be associated not with the prose fiction which during the eighteenth and nineteenth centuries gradually became the dominant literary form in England, but with older 'philosophical' works. By this is meant not books by philosophers, like Hobbes or Locke, but works which imaginatively present views of the world to thinking men, such as Rabelais' satire, the *Utopia* of Sir Thomas More, Milton's *Paradise Lost*, or Johnson's *Rasselas*. Swift and the educated audience of his day were connoisseurs of argument. If they were university men, they had undergone a course of study very largely consisting of constructing arguments in disputations, and on both sides of a question, that is, a training in building and judging argument. Even non-university readers (and the *Travels* was a popular book) were used to listening to a set piece of argument at least once a week, in church. Of course, the imaginative greatness of Gulliver's *Travels* (and one of the chief weapons of Swift as a satirist) is the elaboration of the possibility that there may be more than *two* sides to an argument. The savage power of his satire seems to come partly from the tension between this imaginative abundance and his equally strong drive to reduce every question to two sides, his own right one and a wrong one which is assigned to an opponent. This, however, comes back again to his training, because this also is part of the art of disputing. Swift is in constant pursuit of the elusive ideal that a problem ought to be discussed dialectically.'

In each book, Swift may be seen setting up his arguments, a complex process which involves creating a situation, often dramatic and always realised in significant, even symbolic, detail. This has been fruitfully discussed by recent critics using the idea of 'situational satire'. That is, keeping in mind that every statement and argument must be related to its surroundings:—or rather, that the 'idea' cannot be filleted out of the text, but is controlled and conditioned by the circumstances which embody it. The argument itself is carried out by means of language, and so the strange tongues of the 'several Nations' are more than mere decoration. They are a vital part of the imaginative process of the book.

In fact, of course, Swift was obsessed with language. This can be seen
from the private, 'little language', 'ourrichar Gangridge', he evolved and
used in his intimate letters from London, from 1710 to 1714, known in
printed form as the *Journal to Stella*, to the three different Anglo-Latin
languages he worked at with his friend Sheridan later in his life. Both the
'situation' network and the question of language will be discussed later.
To start the argument working, however, Swift creates a *persona* who
will be the protagonist in the dialectical battles, an 'I', 'Mr. *Lemuel
Gulliver* . . born in *Nottinghamshire*, where his Father dwelt . . . distin-
guished for his Veracity'. It is necessary to consider him first.

The establishment of Gulliver, the writer of the Travels, begins in the
framework of the book. 'Richard Sympson' introduces him with the
words quoted above, and Swift carefully gives some crucial facts about
him in the first chapter. He is a younger son of a small country gentle-
man. Thus he is a believable and fairly substantial narrator with some
traditional culture, some moderate tincture of 'breeding'. His father
was able to send him to the university, so that he has some education; his observations are not ignorant. His inheritance makes him
déclassé, however; he cannot inherit his father's land, so he must choose a
profession. Thus he is a little ill at ease in the hierarchical social picture
Swift wishes to discuss in the satire. He chose medicine as a career, but
not the higher, more humane and 'literary' (and more expensive) training
as a physician, rather the more practical, more tradesman-like practice of
surgery, entered through an apprenticeship. This choice is forced on him
by his father's comparative poverty and it makes him slightly dis-
oriented in the hierarchy of intellectual studies. He did get some training
in medicine at Leyden, but there in that cheap, university town, flourished
the very theoretical, speculative, 'Cartesian' school of chemical medicine,
that was led by the famous Boerhaave. This school of investigation was
described as 'Cartesian', because diagnosis and analysis were attempted
on rational, 'mathematical' principles. It was in fact 'scientific' medicine,
instead of a study of the texts of Galen and other ancient doctors, or a
course of reading in the liberal arts. Of course, Gulliver had also earlier
set himself to learn 'Navigation and other parts of Mathematicks'. His
practical bent and professional skill led him to sail as a 'Surgeon success-
ively in two Ships' and he 'made several Voyages for six years, to the
East and *West-Indies*.' On the other hand his general education was not
neglected, for his 'Hours of Leisure' were 'spent in reading the best
Authors, ancient and modern'. What use he makes of this general educa-

tion is another matter. Most usefully for the purpose of setting up Swift's exotic arguments, when Gulliver was among a strange people, he was prompted to learn 'their Language; wherein I had a great Facility by the Strength of my Memory.'

So much for his abilities and the improvement of his intellect. As far as his personal life goes, when he was 'advised to alter his Condition' to make a better figure as a doctor, he 'married Mrs. *Mary Burton*, second Daughter to Mr. *Edmond Burton*, Hosier, in *Newgate-street*', who brought him a small dowry. He is thus emotionally (or temperamentally) as well as intellectually at the disposal of others, a kind of emotional and intellectual shuttlecock. He is married off in the middle station of life to a second daughter, and profits modestly.

Gulliver is not a complete 'patsy' in an argument, but a type of Man himself. Often wrong, sometimes right, suffering from the sin of pride, no doubt, especially intellectual pride which a devotee of mathematical learning might easily acquire from the apparent prestige of that study at the end of the seventeenth century. Nevertheless, he is practical and reasonably competent. In the great chain of being, which God created, man was the mid-point between angel and beast. This humanist picture inherited by Swift is part of the doctrine of Gulliver's *Travels*, and Gulliver is by pride either unaware of his difficult position or directly kicking against it. Pope in his *Essay on Man* neatly sums up the situation:

> Plac'd on this isthmus of a middle state,
> A being darkly wise, and rudely great . . .
> Born but to die and reas'ning but to err;
> Alike in ignorance, his reason such,
> Whether he thinks too little, or too much . . .
> Sole judge of Truth, in endless Error hurl'd:
> The glory, jest, and riddle of the World!   *G's char.*

So Gulliver. He is foolish and wrong-headed. He often gets the worst of an argument or discussion with the philosopher-king in Brobdingnag or with a rational horse, but yet he is in a way admirable. His observation is sometimes careful and just, backed by experience. He quite correctly observes that the philosopher-king of Brobdingnag 'lives wholly secluded from the rest of the World', and that this damages his point of view since he must therefore be 'altogether unacquainted with the Manners and Customs that most prevail in other Nations: The Want of which Knowledge will ever produce many *Prejudices*, and a certain *Narrowness of Thinking*.'

He then, however, rams a Gulliverian conclusion to this: 'from which we and the politer Countries of *Europe* are wholly exempted'. In chapter 3 of the fourth Voyage, the Yahoos are alleged by Gulliver's Houyhnhnm master to be 'the most unteachable of all Brutes', *and*, in the same paragraph, the same Houyhnhnm

> knew it was impossible that there could be a Country beyond the Sea or that a Parcel of Brutes could move a wooden Vessel whither they pleased upon Water.

This rather neatly brackets Gulliver's abilities and limitations. The horse has no experience or knowledge and in this case reason is useless, so he holds a wrong opinion. Gulliver has experience and knowledge but often reason fails him and he comes to wrong conclusions. His honesty does triumph over his vanity on occasion, and he does rather splendidly survive. The quality of adaptability and his survival mean that there is some point in reading the book as an account of adventures befalling a human being with whom we all feel kinship, but the dangers of that view lie in the arguments Gulliver gets into.

Gulliver is also a 'middle man' in religion. By connecting him with Nottinghamshire and educating him at Emmanuel College, Cambridge (the college of John Harvard, founder of Harvard College in puritan New England), Swift probably intended without making him an extremist to give him a Puritan upbringing. This would sit neatly with his mathematical and Cartesian enthusiasm. If this is true, then he was endowed with a tincture of two attitudes of mind particularly abhorred by Swift. These were, a confidence in personal religious belief, trust in the 'inner light', and a confidence in unaided human reason as evinced in certain scientific speculations and their concommitant economic and social tyranny. The former is one of the objects of satire in *A Tale of a Tub*. The latter is a common attitude of mind for the Swift *persona*. It is most powerfully developed in two of his greatest satirical pieces, *An Argument Against Abolishing Christianity* advanced by an 'emancipated' political speculator and *A Modest Proposal for Preventing the Children of Ireland from being a Burden to their Parents or Country* 'humbly' offered by an arrogant economic reasoner.

From this it can be seen that the complexity of the way in which the satire is carried on partly arises from the employment of a *persona* in situations of satirical argument. Gulliver is, like man himself, inconsistent. There is no development in the 'character' of Gulliver. His desperate

wish to be a horse at the end of the book is as foolish as his feeling of
God-like superiority to the Lilliputians based on nothing better than his
physical size. There is, however, a development in the difficulty of the
writing, towards a denser argument, because of the experience the
reader has had in the first three books.

Gulliver, the *persona*, also acts as a kind of refractor of the experiences
offered to him. He is in many ways representative. If we despise him, it
is because we fail to see ourselves in him. The inconsistent attitudes he
adopts might each one be an attitude we could on occasion adopt ourselves. It is the skill of the satire to show the attitudes in an ironical light,
to present each piece of description, each argument so that the reader
can, if he is alert, see several possibilities. As a refractor, who splits up the
white light of our experience into the constituent colours of the moralist's
concern, Gulliver is a type of Man himself, on his 'Isthmus of a middle
State, A being darkly wise'.

One of the most widely known and quoted passages in the book is the
king of Brobdingnag's judgement on Gulliver's fellow Europeans as

> the most pernicious Race of little odious Vermin that Nature ever
> suffered to crawl upon the Surface of the Earth.

This judgement has been on occasion grossly misinterpreted as Swift's
misanthropic opinion of mankind, but in the context of argument, the
situation is quite complex. First of all, of course, it is the king's opinion.
He specifically says that from Gulliver's own 'Relation and the Answers
[that he has] with much Pains wringed and extorted', he 'cannot but
conclude' this. That is, Gulliver's argumentative performance provokes
the judgement. There is uncertainty about the truth of Gulliver's 'Relation' and 'Answers', and further uncertainty about whether the king
has reasonably drawn this conclusion. Finally the reader's response must
take in account how ineptly Gulliver performs in answering the king's
questions. He performs badly through pride, obtuseness and dishonesty.
This is beautifully and ironically shown in his own stuffy comment:

> IMAGINE with thy self, courteous Reader, how often I then wished
> for the Tongue of *Demosthenes* or *Cicero*, that might have enabled me
> to celebrate the Praise of my own dear native Country in a Style equal
> to its Merits and Felicity.

Here Gulliver begins with the rhetoric of an insinuating author and
incautiously invokes the good rhetoric of two great orators of antiquity

who truthfully castigated their own society. Gulliver finally ends by equating 'Style' with expedient persuasion. The king's own remark, however, is open to modification. Gulliver has earlier correctly observed to him 'That, Reason did not extend itself with the Bulk of the Body', and that the Brobdingnagians are a 'People . . . wholly excluded from any Commerce with the rest of the World'. Later, when Gulliver offers 'as a small Tribute of Acknowledgment' to make twenty or thirty guns and a supply of powder and ammunition capable of supporting by force the king's 'absolute Commands', the latter is 'struck with Horror'. Gulliver appears to him as an 'impotent and groveling' insect with a fiendish imagination. But Gulliver is not 'impotent and groveling', though perhaps the king feels that for his size he should be. Here the king is as heedless as Gulliver in Lilliput. On the other hand the king also acts at times as a spokesman for Swift. He puts forward a traditional, anti-Machiaevellian view of statecraft, which Swift himself held and propounded:

> For, I remember very well, in a Discourse one Day with the King; when I happened to say, there were several thousand Books among us written upon the *Art of Government*; it gave him (directly contrary to my Intention) a very mean Opinion of our Understandings. He professed both to abominate and despise all *Mystery, Refinement*, and *Intrigue*, either in a Prince or a Minister. He could not tell what I meant by *Secrets of State*, where an Enemy or some Rival Nation were not in the Case. He confined the Knowledge of governing within very *narrow Bounds*; to common Sense and Reason, to Justice and Lenity, to the Speedy Determination of Civil and criminal Causes . . .

The king attacks Gulliver's point of view by restating it using a number of abusive terms such as *Art of Government* (in its bad sense), *Mystery, Refinement, Intrigue, Secrets of State*. The king's restatement is from the point of view of a specific argument about the nature of government which implied the uselessness of political parties and political dispute. The general satire has thus an added particular level which forces close attention to judgements of speakers like the king.

In Book IV, the complexity of the argument lies largely in defining Gulliver's own point of view. A good example of this is the beginning of chapter 7:

> THE Reader may be disposed to wonder how I could prevail on my self to give so free a Representation of my own Species, among the Race of Mortals who were already too apt to conceive the vilest

Opinion of Human Kind, from that entire Congruity betwixt me and their *Yahoos*. But I must freely confess, that the many Virtues of these excellent *Quadrupeds* placed in opposite View to human Corruptions, had so far opened mine Eyes, and enlarged my Understanding, that I began to view the Actions and Passions of Man in a very different Light; and to think the Honour of my own Kind not worth managing; which, besides, it was impossible for me to do before a Person of so acute a Judgement as my Master, who daily convinced me of a thousand Faults in my self, whereof I had not the least Perception before, and which with us would never be numbered among human Infirmities. I had likewise learned from his Example an utter Detestation of all Falsehood or Disguise; and *Truth* appeared so amiable to me, that I determined upon sacrificing every thing to it.

So far, so good, except that the 'thousand Faults in my self, whereof I had not the least Perception before' is ironical. Gulliver ought to be able, on most occasions, to see human faults without going for new ones. The following paragraph, however, has the true Gulliver note:

LET me deal so candidly with the Reader, as to confess, that there was yet a much stronger Motive for the Freedom I took in my Representation of Things. I had not been a Year in this Country, before I contracted such a Love and Veneration for the Inhabitants, that I entered on on a firm Resolution never to return to human Kind, but to pass the rest of my Life among these admirable *Houyhnhnms* in the Contemplation and Practice of every Virtue; where I could have no Example or Incitement to Vice. But it was decreed by Fortune, my perpetual Enemy, that so great a Felicity should not fall to my Share. However, it is now some Comfort to reflect, that in what I said of my Countrymen, I *extenuated* their Faults as much as I durst before so strict an Examiner; and upon every Article, gave as *favourable* a Turn as the Matter would bear. For, indeed, who is there alive that will not be swayed by his Byass and Partiality to the Place of his Birth?

We see, again, that the argument will bear narrow observation. Gulliver resolves 'never to return to human kind', an impossible identification with the thinking horses which is later ironically elaborated. He decides to live a life of cloistered virtue with 'no Example or Incitement to Vice'; that is except his own nature, for he then embarks on a misguided justification of his rhetorical exercise in *presenting* European culture in what he thinks to be the fairest light. This is Gulliver's refracting function, for the reasons for his distortion of the truth are the main interest in his point of view. After Gulliver's Conversations, the horse has his say:

[My master] said, he had been very seriously considering my whole Story, as far as it related both to my self and my Country: That, he looked upon us as a Sort of Animals to whose Share, by what Accident he could not conjecture, some small Pittance of *Reason* had fallen, whereof we made no other Use than by its Assistance to aggravate our *natural* Corruptions, and to acquire new ones which Nature had not given us. That, we disarmed our selves of the few Abilities she had bestowed; had been very successful in multiplying our original Wants, and seemed to spend our whole Lives in vain Endeavours to supply them by our own Inventions. That, as to my self, it was manifest I had neither the Strength or Agility of a common *Yahoo*; that I walked infirmly on my hinder Feet. . . .

THAT, our Institutions of *Government* and *Law* were plainly owing to our gross Defects in *Reason*, and by consequence in *Virtue*; because *Reason* alone is sufficient to govern a *Rational* Creature; which was therefore a Character we had no Pretence to challenge, even from the Account I had given of my own People; although he manifestly perceived, that in order to favour them, I had concealed many Particulars, and often *said the Thing which was not.*

This is an argumentative answer to Gulliver's unwary position. Man is a 'sort of Animal' with a 'Pittance of Reason'. Gulliver misuses *his* 'pittance' to present 'favourable' pictures, which receive rational judgement. Human institutions of '*Government* and *Law*' certainly exist to correct human defects (and consequently form the substance of a good part of Swift's work) but only Gulliver would be outflanked on this line. No thoughtful man would claim that he is a completely '*Rational* Creature'. But the argument is not to be taken at face value. Rational horses are not men, and Gulliver's desire to be a horse is the obviously ridiculous correlative of his desire not to accept other limitations of human nature.

· The 'network of situations' governs not only the arguments, but also organises the 'objectifying' descriptions. A famous instance of Swift's powerful talent in this field is the famous passage about the beggars:

A Coach was allowed to Glumdalclitch and me, wherein her Governess frequently took her out to see the Town, or go among the Shops; and I was always of the Party, carried in my Box, . . . I reckoned our Coach to be about a Square of *Westminster-Hall*, but not altogether so High; however, I cannot be very exact. One Day the Governess ordered our Coachman to stop at several Shops; where the Beggars watching their Opportunity, crowded to the Sides of the Coach, and gave me the most horrible Spectacles that ever an *European* Eye beheld. There was a Woman with a Cancer in her Breast, swelled to a monstrous Size, full of Holes, in two or three of which I could easily have crept, and covered my whole Body. There was a fellow with a Wen on his Neck, larger than five Woolpacks; and another with a couple of wooden Legs, each about twenty Foot high. But, the most hateful Sight of all was the Lice crawling on their Cloaths: I could see distinctly the Limbs of these Vermin with my naked Eye, much better than those of an *European* Louse through a Microscope; and their Snouts with which they rooted like Swine.

Here is an example of Swift's 'objectifying' imagination, apparently allied to the loathing of the human body which he is attacked for. It begins like an engraved picture of a street scene. At another level, it is part of the witty exploitation of relative size. The small objects in Lilliput are often described as bigger than something familiar, such as 'a Turret at least five Foot high' or the Emperor, 'taller by almost the Breadth of my Nail, than any of his Court'. In Brobdingnag, things are made smaller, 'about a Square of *Westminster-Hall*, but not altogether so High' or the royal oven 'is not so wide by ten Paces as the Cupola of St. *Paul's*'. This wit is also seen in the nature of the comparisons in the passage itself: 'a Fellow with a Wen on his Neck, larger than five Wool-packs'. This is part of a structure of rural references that runs all through Book II, strengthening the idea of the Brobdingnagian state as a patriar-chal one, rooted in a traditional, healthy, 'good' rural economy. Similar instances are: the king's 'Razor was almost twice as long as an ordinary Scythe'; the queen's 'Knives were twice as long as a Scythe set strait upon the handle'; and so on. To some extent this is also part of the further exploration of relative size, which is one of the themes of the first two books, showing that in moral argument comparison is valuable but size is not. The coach is said, wittily, to be 'a Square of *Westminster-Hall*'. In Westminster Hall, in Swift's day, the courts of justice sat in groups round the walls. Thus a thread of argument is started. Scenes such as the beggars at the shops must have been familiar enough to Gulliver, or any passer-by in London, or Dublin, and the hardship and injustice of their plight should have been no less obvious. The *Size* here, however, makes the spectacle seem to Gulliver, the most horrible 'that ever *European* eye beheld'. Lousy conditions were also common enough in Gulliver's 'own dear native Country'. The famous passage describing Gulliver and the Brobdingnagian maids-of-honour is another instance of Swift's playing about with size, comparison and judgement. Body smell as well as visual appearance is the focus of the passage:

> . . . to say the Truth, a very offensive Smell came from their Skins; which I do not mention or intend to the Disadvantage of those excellent Ladies, for whom I have all Manner of Respect: But, I conceive, that my Sense was more acute in Proportion to my Littleness and that those illustrious Persons were no more disagreeable to their Lovers, or to each other, than People of the same Quality are with us in England. And, after all, I found their natural Smell was much more supportable than when they used Perfumes, under which I immediately swooned away. I cannot forget, that an intimate Friend of mine in Lilliput took the Freedom in a warm Day, when I had used a good deal of Exercise, to complain of a strong Smell about me; although I am as little faulty that way as most of my Sex:

> . . . I was placed on their Toylet directly before their naked Bodies; which, I am sure, to me was very far from being a tempting sight, or from giving me any other Motions than those of Horror and Disgust. Their Skins appeared so coarse and uneven, so variously coloured when I saw them near, with a Mole here and there as broad as a Trencher, and Hairs hanging from it thicker than Pack-threads; to say nothing further concerning the rest of their Persons.

In Swift's rhetorical and 'objectified' satire, language is shown to be one of the least reliable props of human reason, since while it is the embodiment of reason, it is also the vehicle of that reason turned to pride and error, the particularly human failing.

The wise and virtuous *Houyhnhnms*, who abound in all Excellencies that can adorn a rational Creature, have no Name for this Vice in their Language, which hath no Terms to express any thing that is evil, except those whereby they describe the detestable Qualities of their *Yahoos*; among which they were not able to distinguish this of Pride, for want of thoroughly understanding Human Nature, as it sheweth it self in other Countries, where that Animal presides.

Reason is not with the Houyhnhnms, of course,

> . . . a Point problematical as with us, where Men can argue with Plausibility on both Sides of a Question; but strikes you with immediate Conviction; as it must needs do where it is not mingled, obscured, or discoloured by Passion and Interest.

The 'Passion' and 'Interest' in Swift's own language give it life, the reader thinks uneasily. In the texture of his writing, the unreliable nature of language is constantly suggested. Take, for example, his lists such as:

> the very worst Effects that Avarice, Faction, Hypocrisy, Perfidiousness, Cruelty, Rage, Madness, Hatred, Envy, Lust, Malice, and Ambition can produce.

and

> I am not in the least provoked at the Sight of a Lawyer, a Pick-pocket, a Colonel, a Fool, a Lord, a Gamester, a Politician, a Whore-munger, a Physician, an Evidence, a Suborner, an Attorney, a Traytor, or the like. . .

There are terms like *Faction* and *Ambition* in the first and *Colonel, Lord, Physician, Attorney,* in the second, which are out of step with their neighbours, but which by the nature of the language process take colour from the others. Lists of mingled catagories are a feature of all Swift's writing.

So much for the complexity of Swift's satire, which forces the reader to grapple with the text, to be on his guard, and above all, to consider his own position and defences as he reads.

"Situational satire"

"destroying description"

3. The Nature of the Satire: Unity

If the conduct of the satire is complex, and there is little possibility of 'explaining' the book by simply arguing Swift's misanthropy or the like, is there any kind of unity in it? It seems that there may be. The centre of the satire is man himself. Swift, in a shifting kaleidoscope of argument, narrative, wit and imagination, goes over and over the puzzle of man's nature. The topic is man's inner make-up and man's social role.

As has been previously argued, Swift begins from the traditional picture of man's middle state, between the angels and the beasts. Man's faculty of reason, which distinguishes him from the beasts, is the faculty by which he most seriously errs, through pride. He is truly

> The glory, jest and riddle of the world!

Obviously, however, the jest and the riddle in the situation are more congenial to Swift's wit and more appropriate centres for his satirical purposes. The glory, however, is not absent from Swift's vision. Is it not the distance in this picture between the possibility inherent in man and his actual achievement that gives the edge to Swift's savage indignation? The potential of the faculty makes man's corrupt behaviour immeasureably worse. He can rationalise his worst actions instead of accepting blame and censure. His best efforts are in constant danger of being betrayed by his own nature. The very language he uses, so powerful and lively, is apt to throw him into deepest error. This deep preoccupation of Swift's, and of course it is a deep preoccupation of many Christian apologists of his time, produces a unity in the book through Gulliver's point of view, which illustrates it, and at a different level through imagery which symbolises it. Such a preoccupation springs from a view of man which is not exclusively, nor perhaps necessarily Christian. Just as there is little specifically doctrinal argument in the book, so it has had a wider, more general and longer-lasting popularity than, for example, Pope's *Essay on Man*, or Johnson's *Rasselas*.

The tension in man between his animal nature and his reasoning faculty is the source of a part of one of the unifying features in Gulliver's *Travels*, image patterns. Books II and IV are specifically 'animal' books, though of course the rational-animal see-saw is always liable to appear in the other voyages. The imaginative skill and witty humour with which Swift deploys the 'animals' in the narrative is obvious.

Book II teems with animals like the cat, 'three times larger than an Ox', purring like 'a Dozen Stocking-weavers at work'; a 'Mastiff equal in Bulk to four Elephants' and a Greyhound; two Rats with tails 'two Yards long wanting an Inch'; flies, 'each of them as big as a *Dunstable Lark*'; wasps 'as large as Partridges'; lice, rooting in beggars' skin 'like Swine'; 'a small white Spaniel'; a menacing kite; moles that make hills into which Gulliver falls up to his neck; a dangerous snail, whose shell breaks his shin; fearless 'smaller Birds'; a confident and predatory thrush; a pugnacious linnet; a huge frog, 'daubing [Gulliver's] Face and Cloathes with its odious Slime'; a monkey, 'as large as an Elephant' who almost kills Gulliver with kindness. Even 'a Cowdung' is a hazard to an athletic man. Finally Gulliver's escape from Brobdingnag is unintentionally brought about by 'some Eagle' who wants to break Gulliver out of his box, 'like a Tortoise in a Shell'. This is topsy-turvy land with a vengeance. Similarly in Book IV, the Yahoos' animal appearance is attentively and wittily elaborated, and by comparisons with predatory animals and other means, their bestiality carefully established. 'The young Animal's Flesh', for example, smelled 'very rank, and the Stink was somewhat between a *Weasel* and a Fox, but much more disagreeable'; and 'They swim from their Infancy like Frogs.' The traditional, allegorical background of the animals mentioned is important. The horses', the reasoning animals', life is also detailed, and this is often very funny.

> The *Houyhnhnms* use the hollow Part between the Pastern and the Hoof of their Fore-feet, as we do our Hands, and this with greater Dexterity, than I could at first imagine. I have seen a white Mare of our Family thread a Needle (which I lent her on Purpose) with that Joynt . . .

All this, however, is placed within Swift's rhetorical framework. The animal references, descriptions, comparisons and identifications are introduced as a motif in Book II with Swift's usual aggressive intent on the reader. They gain an even more telling argumentative function when they are reintroduced in Book VI.

Among the Brobdingnagians, Gulliver is identified as a helpless, small animal. The first Brobdingnagian who encounters him

... considered a while with the Caution of one who endeavours to lay hold on a small dangerous Animal in such a Manner that it shall not be able either to scratch or bite him; as I my self have sometimes done with a *Weasel* in *England*.

His usually dominant role in relation to the animal world is turned upside down. He is forced to consider his own circumstances from a position of physical inferiority.

[The farmer] called his Hinds about him, and asked them (as I afterwards learned) whether they had ever seen in the Fields any little Creature that resembled me.

His nature is not benevolently regarded by the Brobdingnagians. The farmer's

Wife ... screamed and ran back as Women in *England* do at the Sight of a Toad or a Spider

and he is in some physical danger on account of his insignificant size and *consequent* loss of moral authority

... being afraid the Boy might owe me a Spight; and well remembering how mischievous all Children among us naturally are to Sparrows, Rabbits, young Kittens and Puppy-Dogs; ...

Even at best, he is an animal curiosity, like the emblems on country inn signs.

a strange creature to be seen at the Sign of the Green *Eagle*, not so big as a *Splacknuck*.

The rhetorical framework should be kept in mind because what is constantly being put foward is Gulliver's opinion of his own situation, and the opinions of others (Brobdingnagians and Houyhnhnms) about his nature. Swift's 'meaning' is partly contained in the contrast between these two sets of views, between *situation* and *nature*. The panel of three great Brobdingnagian 'Scholars, who were then in their weekly Waiting' are called in to give 'expert' opinion, and

They all agreed that I could not be produced according to the regular Laws of Nature; because I was not framed with a Capacity of preserving my Life, either by Swiftness, or climbing of Trees, or digging Holes in the Earth. They observed by my Teeth, which they viewed with great Exactness, that I was a carnivorous Animal; yet most

Quadrupeds being an Overmatch for me; and Field-Mice, with some others, too nimble, they could not imagine how I should be able to support my self, unless I fed upon Snails and other insects; which they offered by many learned Arguments to evince that I could not possibly do.

The king observed:

how contemptible a Thing was human Grandeur, which could be mimicked by such diminutive Insects as I: And yet, said he, I dare engage, those Creatures . . . contrive little Nests and Burrows, that they call Houses and Cities . . .

Gulliver, however, is permitted the reasonable comment 'That, Reason did not extend itself with the Bulk of the Body', and while being forced physically to submit to animal attack and even (as in the case of the monkey) dangerous animal affection, denies the conclusions the Brobdingnagians came to. The philosopher-king's famous statement

I cannot but conclude the Bulk of your Natives, to be the most pernicious Race of little odious Vermin that Nature ever suffered to crawl upon the Surface of the Earth

is rather sharply qualified by the animal-image structure of the book, not by any direct intervention of Swift himself.

In Book IV, Gulliver's Houyhnhnm Master is given an opinion about Gulliver, as an animal, a Yahoo 'endued with Reason'.

. . . considering the Frame of our Bodies, and especially of mine, he thought no Creature of equal Bulk was so ill-contrived, for employing that Reason in the common Offices of Life, . . . in point of real Advantage, he thought I differed [from the other Yahoos] for the worse. That my Nails were of no Use either to my fore or hinder Feet: As to my fore Feet, he could not properly call them by that Name, for he never observed me to walk upon them; that they were too soft to bear the Ground, . . . That I could not walk with any Security; for if either of my hinder Feet slipped. I must inevitably fall. He then began to find Fault with other Parts of my Body; . . .

It can be seen again, that the animal-image elaboration of human life, set within almost unimaginable ironic complexity in this book, produces 'conclusions' on the part of some important interlocutor that need severe qualification. 'In point of real Advantage', says the thinking horse, a dangerous phrase in Swift's rhetoric.

At the level of philosophical doctrine, Swift is obviously playing with the notion of man's 'middle state', half way between angels and beasts. As Pope says, however, if man is

> In doubt to deem himself a God or Beast;
> In doubt his Mind or Body to prefer . . .[1]

any *preference* is wrong. He is neither God nor Beast, but in the uneasy state of being Man. Swift's animal imagery, either locally by conceits or at length in the book, by structure, is a constant commentary on the 'Chaos of Thought and Passion, all confus'd' that the middle state entails.

The structure of animal imagery also preserves the ironic distance which Swift is careful to keep round the Houyhnhnms, so that they are not, by careful readers, seen as models for human conduct. Gulliver is wrong to take them as such. That is, on occasion they may propound arguments which are correct, but man cannot *imitate* them. Neither are they wholly to be seen as representing 'deists', 'stoics', or some other kind of sectaries who are wrong, or to be attacked, and as such the victims of Swiftian satire. They are inhuman, completely rational, and, though a man might envy their calm, unclouded judgement, he cannot expect constantly to enjoy their advantages. The Yahoos have a life that the Houyhnhnms lack. The horses' spectral culture is neatly outlined:

THE *Houyhnhnms* have no Letters, and consequently, their Knowledge is all traditional. But there happening few Events of any Moment among a People so well united, naturally disposed to every Virtue, wholly governed by Reason, and cut off from all Commerce with other Nations; the historical Part is easily preserved without burthening their Memories. I have already observed, that they are subject to no Diseases, and therefore can have no Need of Physicians. However, they have excellent Medicines composed of Herbs . . .

IN *Poetry* they must be allowed to excel all other Mortals; wherein the Justness of their Similes, and the Minuteness, as well as Exactness of their Descriptions, are indeed inimitable. Their Verses abound very much in both of these; and usually contain either some exalted Notions of Friendship and Benevolence, or the Praises of those who were Victors in Races, and other bodily Exercises.

Everything about them is admirable but simplified. They are 'wholly governed by Reason'; Gulliver also jams into that paragraph the fact that they are 'subject to no Diseases'. Are just similes, and minute and exact descriptions the high points of the poet's art? Of course this may tell us more about Gulliver's literary judgement than about the Houyhnhnms' culture. The last few lines of the quotation present an ironic juxtaposition of ideas surely meant to present the horses with some irony: exalted notions *or* praises of athletes, both, Gulliver seems to say, are equally good to the quadruped sages.

A man does not live to himself, however, and his social nature is equally important to Swift. Gulliver who in many ways is a typical man, typical of Swift and the reader as well, travels *into* several remote nations and his reports are much concerned with political, social and economic concerns. In distinction to the 'animal' books, II and IV, the first Voyage, and the Voyage to Laputa in Book III, may be described as 'mechanical'.

Because of his size, Gulliver sees the Lilliputian economy as an intricate machine, comprehensible because of its scale. The man-mountain, again because of his size, engages the whole apparatus of the Lilliputian state:

> IN the mean time, the Emperor held frequent Councils to debate what Course should be taken with me; . . . an Imperial Commission was issued out, obliging all the Villages nine hundred Yards round the City, to deliver in every Morning six Beeves, forty Sheep [etc.] . . . his Majesty gave Assignments upon his Treasury. . . .

Swift is able wittily to employ the knowledge of forms of Government administration, such as the Articles of Impeachment, which he had acquired while he was a friend of the men in power in London in the years between 1710 and 1714.

As well as the social organisations of the little men, 'the *Hurgo* and his Train', the Blefuscan fleet, and so on, Swift stresses the mechanical ingenuity of the inhabitants. The first chapter ends with the description of the 'machine' which a group of clever artificers contrive for moving the Man-Mountain:

> THESE People are most excellent Mathematicians, and arrived to a great Perfection in Mechanicks by the Countenance and Encourage-ment of the Emperor, who is a renowned Patron of Learning. This Prince hath several Machines fixed on Wheels for the Carriage of Trees and other great Weights. He often buildeth his largest Men of War, whereof some are Nine Foot long, in the Woods where the Timber grows, and has them carried on these Engines three or four Hundred Yards to the Sea. Five Hundred Carpenters and Engineers

were immediately set at work to prepare the greatest Engine they had. It was a Frame of Wood raised three Inches from the Ground, about seven Foot long and four wide, moving upon twenty two Wheels. . . . But the principal Difficulty was to raise and place me in this Vehicle. Eighty Poles, each of one Foot high, were erected for this Purpose, and very strong Cords of the bigness of Pack-thread were fastened by Hooks to many Bandages, which the Workman had girt round my Neck, my Hands, my Body and my Legs. Nine hundred of the Strongest Men were employed to draw up these Cords by many Pullies. . . .

Here the social mechanism, the Emperor's patronage of mathematics, the witty detail of comparison and measurement, and mechanical ingenuity are all allied.

Such passages allow Gulliver, the mathematician and practical man, to admire the efficiency of the Lilliputians, but also present the moral problems of state action acutely. Chapter 7, the account of the intrigue to impeach Gulliver, is an instance of this. The chapter contains the actual 'Articles of Impeachment', that is, the mechanism for dealing with Gulliver. The 'Articles' are given a background of mechanistic ingenuity which also emphasises the chilling, inhuman cruelty of the compromise reached at the Council Table to blind Gulliver. Here man's reason is being inhumanly, or inhumanely, cruel. The political level of 'meaning' in this Voyage, the Walpole-Flimnap passages for example, is central to the whole book and not solely one of Swift's hobby-horses, or an expression of personal political spleen. Swift constantly attacks the 'new' concept of party-politics and government by party strife, which was often seen as engineered by 'managers' like Walpole. The very first 'original' book he ever printed, the *Discourse of the Contests and Dissensions between the Nobles and Commons in Athens and Rome* (1701) presents the same view of politics. Swift always believed that events were, and should be, caused by particular men, but he held an old-fashioned view of the 'unreasonableness', if inevitability of 'faction'. This is dangerously close to presenting his own view as central, rational, common-sensical and 'right' and any opposing view as peripheral, irrational and wrong. Thus he does not need to argue it down, but can amply and nimbly satirise it. He advances in place of what we should accept as the development of party government a traditional, hierarchic notion of the state governed by 'natural' leaders, the notion put forward by the king of Brobdingnag. This view is associated in several of his works with metaphors of 'the body politic' and other 'natural' figures. In his attack on 'party' he associates the ideas he wishes to discredit with cruel, 'mechanical' intrigue, or if not cruel then heedless and unfeeling action which results in tyranny. The ambition that fires men to succeed unscrupulously in politics is a form of misdirected reason, and another dangerous, anti-social function of that pride which comes from misdirected reasoning. The mostly admirable king of Brobdingnag, though not treated without irony, is the ruler of a state without much political machinery. The state of Brobdingnag, moreover is associated with a network of agricultural and patriarchal imagery. There is cruelty in it, but it is on balance good. The horses are associated too with a similar, 'natural' state. While the king, however, is actually made to expound a serious and complex state doctrine, the simplified economy of the horses prevents us from identifying much political doctrine in their comments on Gulliver, except in the general way appropriate to moral discussion. It is in this way that Book IV is harder to interpret than the earlier Voyages.

The beginning of Book III, the Voyage to Laputa, gives us the most elaborate 'mechanical' image of the state. Here the actual functioning of the government depends on managing the flying island and its lodestones. This allows an ironical comparison to be made with the political situation in which Ireland was 'managed' from the remote, alien and oppressive centre of power in London. This again, however, is done in a way that is central to the book's controlling vision, Swift's picture of Man. He is not just producing a pro-Ireland pamphlet. The Laputa-Balnibarbi situation, as the impasse between England and Ireland, is seen as allowing free scope for misapplied reason in social, political and economic matters where bright ideas solely motivated by self-interest seem better than the traditional values of good government—responsibility duty, compassion and love, informed by intelligence. Hence, the satire on the abuses of learning is properly located in this book. The Grand Academy of Lagado is full of projectors, whose ideas have disastrous social implications, since they are likely to be backed by irresponsible power or to appear as the febrile activity of a decayed society:

> The only Inconvenience is, that none of these Projects are yet brought to Perfection; and in the mean time, the whole Country lies miserably waste, the Houses in Ruins, and the People without Food or Cloaths. By all which, instead of being discouraged, they are Fifty Times more violently bent upon prosecuting their Schemes, driven equally by Hope and Despair: . . .

The projectors swindle their fellow men. This is the point for Swift; not that they are 'wrong', or follow exploded ideas. The satire is thus not so learned as that other satire on false ideas, *The Memoirs of Scriblerus*, and if the Voyage to Laputa is read solely as piece of 'intellectual history', an attack on the 'new science', it is not very convincing. Since a number of Swift's associated meanings have dwindled in importance or immediate applicability, this is how the Voyage tends to be read.

This part of the book contains one of the very few spokesmen who are treated without irony:

> THIS Lord *Munodi* was a Person of the first Rank, and had been some Years Governor of *Lagado*; but by a Cabal of Ministers was discharged for Insufficiency. However the king treated him with Tenderness, as a well-meaning Man, but of a low contemptible Understanding.

In travelling through Balnibarbi, which has all the marks of Ireland, Gulliver observes that he

> never knew a Soil so unhappily cultivated, Houses so ill-contrived and so ruinous, or a People whose Countenances and Habit expressed so much Misery and Want. . . .

> But, in three Hours travelling, the Scene was wholly altered; we came into a most beautiful Country; Farmers Houses at small Distances, neatly built, the Fields enclosed, containing Vineyards, Corngrounds and Meadows. Neither do I remember to have seen a more delightful Prospect. His Excellency observed my Countenance to clear up; he told me with a Sigh, that there his Estate began. . . .

So that Munodi comes to be a representative figure, the enlightened patrician, the patriarchal landowner who lives on his own estate, which in its order and efficiency is a microcosm of good human existence. This is the ancient, classical ideal celebrated in England by Ben Jonson amongst others:

> How blest art thou, canst love the country, Wroth,
> Whether by choice, or fate, or both;
> And, though so neere the citie, and the court,
> Art tane with neithers vice, nor sport: . . .
> But canst, at home, in thy securer rest,
> Live, with un-bought provision blest;
> Free from proud porches, or their guilded roofes,
> 'Mongst loughing heards, and solide hoofes:
> Along'st the curled woods and painted meades
> from *To Sir Robert Wroth*

This is the ideal set against disorder caused by certain persons who returned from Laputa

> with a very little Smattering in Mathematicks, but full of Volatile Spirits acquired in that Airy Region . . . [and who] began to dislike the Management of every thing below; . . .

All this reinforces the judgements invited by the projectors of the Academy, and even those provoked by the picture of the really skilled speculators in Laputa, with their flappers.

Swift's attachment to his ideal may be a little nostalgic, which sits ill with his bitter irony. After all, his patriarchal picture as far as Ireland went was based on the ascendancy of the protestant English colonisers, cut off from the people by differencies in race, history and religion, supported in their power by one of the most vicious sets of penal laws in Europe. As a member of the alien religious establishment he was himself squarely in this problem. Similarly he must have viewed the settled, English manifestation of this hierarchic picture as a kind of disinherited younger son.

Book III contains two other voyages, to Glubbdubdrib and to Luggnagg. At first sight this may seem to make the third book into a kind of rag-bag of ideas. All three voyages, however, have at least one related theme, that of man's use of his part, the true purpose of history. To this, of course, Swift attaches the powerful ideas which found expression in the Ancients and Moderns controversy which had agitated intellectuals around 1700. One of Swift's earliest works, *The Battle of the Books*, written in 1674 and published in 1704, was a blow in this argument. The controversy in England was not solely learned or literary, whatever it may have been in France, but had ramifications in science and politics. Swift, following his patron and employer, the retired diplomat and dilletante scholar, Sir William Temple, took the part of the Ancients. He saw ancient, that is Greek and Latin, literature as embodying a hard core of humane truths which later thought and speculation, however, ingenious, could amplify but not disturb, much less overturn. In religious controversy, this sometimes developed into an exclusive division between Christian doctrine and the 'new' or 'cartesian' science; Gulliver has his place with the latter. In politics, there was a division between conservative thinking based on precedent and 'mythic' history on the one hand, and on the other more extreme, innovating, 'rationalistic' ideas. In all this, for personal, Irish, religious reasons, Swift was a conservative of a kind. He might therefore be inclined to argue that history could provide a control for the excesses of unbridled 'reason', by preserving a store of moral lessons.

In Glubbdubrib, the Island of Sorcerers, Gulliver's host, the Governor, produces a pageant of men from the past. This is in line with Swift's notions that the transactions of public life are to be connected with individual action. Gulliver finds out, however, that history must be read very carefully and that there appears to be a radical difference between ancient historical accounts and modern narratives. The former are apparently to be trusted, the latter are more unreliable. In any case, the *moral* heroes of Antiquity, Brutus and other

> Destroyers of Tyrants and Usurpers and Restorers of Liberty to oppressed and injured Nations

excelled more modern heroes, identified by historians with 'kings with their Ancestors'. In the same way Gulliver

> . . . desired that the Senate of *Rome* might appear before me in one large Chamber, and a modern Representative, in Counterview, in another. The first seemed to be an Assembly of Heroes and Demy-Gods; the other a Knot of Pedlars, Pick-Pockets, Highwaymen and Bullies.

Another instructive contrast is between Homer and Aristotle, 'those Antients, who were most renowned for Wit and Learning', and close on their heels, Descartes and Gassendi. When these moderns expound their 'new' systems, Aristotle

> . . . freely acknowledged his own Mistakes in Natural Philosophy [Physics], because he proceeded in many things upon Conjecture, as all Men must do; and he found, that *Gassendi*, who had made the Doctrine of *Epicurns* as palatable as he could, and the *Vortices* of *Descartes*, were equally exploded. He predicted the same Fate to *Attraction* [Newton's notion of Gravity], whereof the present Learned are such zealous Asserters. He said, that new Systems of Nature were but new Fashions, which would vary in every Age; and even those who pretend to demonstrate them from Mathematical Principles, would flourish but a short period of Time, and be out of Vogue when that was determined.

Here is the meeting place of two of the strands of Book III: history and the value of scientific doctrine. Later, the corrupting political effects of luxury are the main lesson to be learned from the historical excursus.

This is an ancient theme which closely involves the eighteenth-century preoccupation with the social function of man, and naturally arises from the application of man's reason to the past, which is embodied in history as an art.

Some of this reads like old material worked into the book; perhaps sketches and characters, aphorisms and hints, but the controlling potential of history, truly interpreted, appears elsewhere in the satire. An attack is made on

> . . . the Roguery and Ignorance of those who pretend to write *Anecdotes* or secret History; . . .

and Gulliver reports from Brobdingnag that

> THE Learning of this People is very defective; consisting only in Morality, History, Poetry and Mathematicks. . . .

where, by Swift's usual tactic of saying the opposite of what he himself believes, history is obviously to be prized.

The Voyage to Luggnagg brings Gulliver into contact with the immortal Struldbruggs. When he first hears of them he

> . . . could not forbear breaking out into Expressions perhaps a little too extravagant. I cryed out as in a Rapture; Happy Nation, where every Child hath at least a Chance for being immortal! Happy People who enjoy so many living Examples of antient Virtue, and have Masters ready to instruct them in the Wisdom of all former Ages! . . .

Just as history is mis-written and mis-read, leaving man without a sure, recorded guide, so human nature cannot bear immortality without the decay of memory. The decay of this recording faculty is objectified by Swift in his famous descriptions of the bodily dilapidations of the Struldbruggs. Thus mankind is firmly placed in a truly 'doubtful state', lacking sure reason, reliable memory and impeccable history.

The case of the Struldbruggs, like that of the Yahoos, raises the problem with Gulliver's *Travels*, that the animal imagery and associations are so much more powerful than the other images. It is certainly true that the power in those figures of senility and bestiality shows some obsessive side of Swift's character. They also strike an answering note in most modern readers. Thus the one half of Swift's concern, the nature of man's inner being, is felt to be the central concern of the book. This fits in with modern explorations of psychology and the concern of modern art with the inner life. Swift, however, is also deeply concerned with social man. It is the case that Swift's picture of the warring forces in man's heart and his presentation of the feebleness and unreliability of reason are congenial, familiar and attractive to the modern reader, while his social doctrine is remote, something to be learned about, even repellent. With the changes in European culture since the end of the eighteenth century, and despite the reaction of fascism, his picture of society has become unfamiliar, hardly more than a historical scheme. This is nowhere more noticeable than in his passages on education in Book I, chapter 6, and Book IV, chapter 8:

[The Lilliputians'] Notions relating to the Duties of Parents and Children differ extremely from ours. For, since the Conjunction of Male and Female is founded upon the great Law of Nature, in order to propagate and continue the Species; the *Lilliputians* will needs have it, that Men and Women are joined together like other Animals, by the Motives of Concupiscence; and that their Tenderness towards their Young proceedeth from the like natural Principle: For which Reason they will never allow, that a Child is under any Obligation to his Father for begetting him, or to his Mother for bringing him into the World; . . . Upon these, and the like Reasonings, their Opinion is, that Parents are the last of all others to be trusted with the Education of their own Children: And therefore they have in every Town public Nurseries, . . .

IN educating the Youth of both Sexes, [the Houyhnhnms'] Method is admirable, and highly deserveth our Imitation. . . .

TEMPERANCE, *Industry*, *Exercise* and *Cleanliness*, are the Lessons equally enjoyed to the young ones of both Sexes: And my Master thought it monstrous in us to give the Females a different kind of Education from the Males, except in some Articles of Domestick Management; whereby, as he truly observed, one Half of our Natives were good for nothing but bringing Children into the World: And to trust the Care of their Children to such useless Animals, he said was yet a greater Instance of Brutality.

Neither of these passages is without irony. Yet, despite the apparently modern idea of giving both sexes a more or less similar education, the impersonality of the educative process which Swift apparently endorses grates on the modern reader's ears! His rigid idea of a stratified society is paralleled in his educational suggestions and in the scheme for financing the Lilliputian state nurseries. This may be a slender example, but it shows the difficulties in the way of responding adequately to more complex issues such as the true well-being of the commonwealth.

D

Conclusion

Swift's great satire may be seen as a controlled display of man's nature and his social life. It presents Swift's vision of the essential contradictions of human nature, of the war between rational control and animal drive, between just judgement and pride (the misdirection of reason), between ignorance and knowledge, between true belief and illusion, between freedom and tyranny. It may well be, that Swift, the Dean and patriot, had answers to some of this. He called himself in his famous epitaph *strenuus libertatis vindicator*, and *liberty* here is to be interpreted quite widely, as political, intellectual and in his own eighteenth-century sense, spiritual. From his pamphlets, his letters and his actions, we may gather various specific remedies which he advocated for human and social ills. Not all of these are to our eyes admirable, or even reasonable. We may think that his political opponents on occasion had at least as much good argument on their side as he had. His position, too, in Ireland, as an officer in a numerically insignificant minority church, shackled to a ruthless alien power structure by its desire to be dominant is clearly indefensible to most modern readers.

The satirist, however, is more than the Dean, and greater than the patriot. Swift's conscious intentions probably arise from his Anglican rationalism; they are probably strengthened by his Church of Ireland conservatism. In all this he follows his role as an eighteenth-century Christian priest and moralist. Gulliver's *Travels*, however, is as a work, not just a parable to 'illustrate' these conscious arguments. The book is a series of patterns forced upon and breasting a turbulent current of feeling and wit. The patterns show Swift's supreme rhetorical skill. The feeling and wit are forces of great power, the marks of Swift's genius. The result is an effect of what might be described as strenuous uncertainty. It is to this that readers have always responded, and in this sense Gulliver's *Travels* transcends the quarrels, preoccupations, politics, controversies, beliefs of Swift's own day, and even of his own faith. The specific facts of Swift's Christianity, of his Irish situation, his Toryism, his intellectual conservatism are ingredients in the satire. The reader ought to know something about them, but they do not control the book. The strenuous uncertainty is the province of the reader. To it Swift contributes the stresses of his own turbulent personality, his love of argument, his skill, wit and his profound suspicions of 'new ideas', of science, even of language itself. The reader contributes the powerful responses, the aroused intellect and feeling, which Swift provokes.

A good instance of how this works is to be found in Swift's so-called scatalogical writing, which occurs only to a limited extent in Gulliver's *Travels*, but which, however, caused serious excisions to be made in nineteenth-century texts of the work, and even in school editions of our own day. A discussion of Swift's 'obsession' with defecation, ordure and so on gets into assessments of his personality, and cannot be dealt with by simply saying that eighteenth-century writers were earthier than later authors. The disturbance to the reader is the real subject, difficult and worth investigation.

Forced against this profound uncertainty is a traditional or accepted point of view. The order lies in the pattern of the book, the disorder comes from 'the darkness within'. Swift allows the play of this order and disorder in the book; perhaps he had no choice, since this may delve deeply into his own being. In his political pamphlets, even in his historical writing, Swift feels obliged to present himself as omniscient and infallible. Naturally this has attracted psychological comment, which sees Swift desperately trying to give substance to the judgements of his super-ego. In Gulliver's *Travels*, however, we may ask, what *is* the author's point of view? From his other works, we can read into the *Travels* what we deduce about his views. This is up to a point quite legitimate. But the total impression left with the reader is rather a tension between personal uncertainty and traditional pictures of order, or between rebellious wit and acceptance. Also, by speaking partly, or mostly, through a *persona*, Swift is relieved from keeping up a consistent authorial voice. In his satires this procedure always seems to release his greatest powers.

He need not be thought to have a 'secret message', nor need his public doctrine be considered as exhaustive of the possibilities within the book. By accepting human nature as it is, in his uncertainty, whatever order he may create from time to time in the book, or whatever doctrine he may believe to answer this uncertainty, he is himself in the satire. This is one of the strengths of the famous Swiftian irony. Of course, he also satirises his own work, in an obvious way, when he talks about the 'little old Treatise, which lay in *Glumdalclitch's* Bedchamber':

> The Book treats of the Weakness of Human kind; and is in little Esteem except among Women and the Vulgar. However, I was

curious to see what an Author of that Country could say upon such a Subject. This Writer went through all the usual Topicks of *European* Moralists; shewing how diminutive, contemptible, and helpless an Animal was Man in his own Nature; how unable to defend himself from Inclemencies of the Air, or the Fury of wild Beasts: How much he was excelled by one Creature in Strength, by another in Speed, by a third in Foresight, by a fourth in Industry. He added, that Nature was degenerated in these latter declining Ages of the World, and could now produce only small abortive Births in Comparison of those in ancient Times. He said, it was very reasonable to think, not only that the Species of Man were originally much larger, but also that there must have been Giants in former Ages; which, as it is asserted by History and Tradition, so it hath been confirmed by huge Bones and Sculls casually dug up in several Parts of the Kingdom, far exceeding the common dwindled Race of Man in our Days. He argued, that the very Laws of Nature absolutely required weshould have been made in the Beginning, of a Size more large and robust, not so liable to Destruction from every little Accident of a Tile falling from an House, or a Stone cast from the Hand of a Boy, or of being drowned in a little Brook. From this Way of Reasoning the Author drew several moral Applications useful in the Conduct of Life, but needless here to repeat. For my own Part, I could not avoid reflecting, how universally this Talent was spread of drawing Lectures in Morality, or indeed rather Matter of Discontent and repining, from the Quarrels we raise with Nature. And, I believe upon a strict Enquiry, those Quarrels might be shown as ill-grounded among us, as they are among that People.

This is not Swift's final view of his book, obviously, but it is an instance of the way he goes round and round various ways of looking at the judgements that appear in his satire.

Another example of a pattern which draws attention to some important feature of the work is the contrast between the four ways in which Gulliver is isolated among the Lilliputians, the Brobdingnagians, the Laputans and the Houyhnhnms. Of course, for the sake of the narrative skeleton, Swift had to get him isolated somehow, and too much may be made of pushing this pattern. There does seem to be, however, some progression in the way Swift has ordered the events.

In the first Voyage, an unavoidable accident, 'a violent Storm', the lot of the Sailor, is responsible for driving the *Antelope* on a rock and destroying her. No failure of skill or courage was responsible. The 'Wind was so strong' that nothing could be done, and 'a sudden Flurry from the North' finished off the ship's boat with the five survivors, leaving Gulliver.

At the opening of the second Voyage, nautical skill is emphasised in the parody of technical discourse, but when the *Adventure* finds herself near a creek, an entirely justified, or at least understandable, failure of nerve leads the landing party to abandon Gulliver, who has become separated. They flee before the 'huge Creature', their failure is moral, not technical, but the event is partly chance.

The fate of the sloop, this time under Gulliver's actual command, at the beginning of the third Voyage, is more complex. On a trading trip, detached from the main business of loading the *Hopewell*, the sloop is captured by pirates, broken men whose hand was against every man's sailing under the more-or-less civilised conventions of the mercantile world. The pirates were often skilled sailors and obviously set little store by their own lives. They had a kind of order or government in the co-operative venture of sailing a ship, which was yet of dubious status because lacking the sanction of legal or religious authority. The fascination of the strange moral world of piracy persists to our own day. Defoe wrote an elaborate *General History of the Pirates*, with an interesting socio-economic preface. Modern literature on the pirates seems largely to come from amateur historians, that is writers who are more concerned perhaps with moral judgements. The use of 'frontier law' in westerns, simplified 'moral' tales, is a parallel case. Swift complicates the pirate picture, however, by introducing the Dutch captain, whose behaviour reaches the extreme of 'heathen' cruelty, and the Japanese captain whose pagan clemency is in marked contrast. Here the wickedness of human nature, perversely issuing in order, but the order of organised rapine and dangerous cruelty, is the cause of Gulliver's isolation.

When Voyage Four opens, Gulliver is no longer a surgeon, or a subordinate officer, but has accepted 'an advantageous Offer . . . to be Captain of the *Adventure*'. Several of his crew die of fever, however, and he recruits men in '*Barbadoes* and the *Leeward Islands*'. Most of these men had been buccaneers, and they corrupt the rest of his crew, so that command of the ship is usurped by mutineers, who decide to turn to piracy. Captain Gulliver is got out of the way by being marooned 'on a Strand' of unknown location. The mutineers are evidently no navigators. Their conduct is not all bad, however, so far as distinctions may be made in such evil-doing, since they don't actually kill him, and they allow him to take some of his belongings without searching him or robbing him further. Gulliver's last isolation is the product of mingled and inefficient human conduct, a great deal of evil, some inefficiency, some good, and some chance. The danger comes to him from within his own 'society', from mutiny, which is still the most feared and heavily punished of seafaring crimes. The theme of betrayal of trust is perhaps underlined by two of the rare appearances of the names of Gulliver's companions: the surgeon, 'Robert Purefoy' 'pure faith' and 'James Welch', one of the mutineers, perhaps with a racialist overtone of thievery. The theme of betrayal runs throughout the entire voyage, as in the discussions about lawyers at the end of chapter 5, and about money at the beginning of chapter 6, as well as in the curious 'embellishment' of a quotation from Virgil, which Gulliver introduces as a piece of 'fine writing' in chapter 12:

> —Nec si miserum Fortuna Sinonem
> Finxit vanum etiam mendacemque improba finget.[1]

This is apt as a quotation (showing that Gulliver has 'read' Virgil) which unites unhappiness (that he isn't a horse), with a refusal to lie (so claiming some of the Houyhnhnms' virtue). Unfortunately, the speech is itself a lie in Virgil's poem, and Sinon with whom Gulliver has ineptly linked himself is the Greek betrayer of Troy, who succeeded in gaining entrance into the city for the wooden horse.

Laying aside this complicated little joke of Swift's, however, there seems to be a progression in the events of the four narratives of isolation, a progression from chance to understandable failure, to external evil, to inner betrayal. The betrayal is also mingled with chance, as in the death of crew-men by fever, and mixed with unskilfulness. Gulliver is rather naïve as a commander not to know that men picked up by chance in the West Indies were likely to be buccaneers. Does this add up to a 'secret message', that inner betrayal, the corruption of reason for example, is the worst fate of man? It might; or perhaps the consciousness of pattern, the threat of the author's continuous presence, is the only sure 'meaning' here, the constant idea of the play of Swift's wit. There is also the feeling received from a consideration of these opening paragraphs of each Voyage, that Book IV is not the end of a 'story', or the centre of the real 'meaning', but a more complex statement of the 'meaning', led up to by the other books.

Swift, the satirist, in Gulliver's Travels forces the reader to bear hard up against the conflict between the possibilities for good in man, and the despicable actions which history, experience and self-realisation all show

---

[1] Although Fortune has made Sinon unhappy, she has not in her malice succeeded in making him a cheat and a liar.

to us. This sad picture is only too certain, only too obvious, yet there is some qualified hope in the work. The past presents the picture of failure, but failure cannot exist without some goal or aim which is not achieved. Swift, the Dean, may have such a goal in plain view, but the Satirist's conclusion, after all the wit and the power, is uncertain. That the satire works seems to be shown by the forcing of unifying patterns on the work by explicators and critics. This is the greatest compliment they can pay to Swift.

Select Bibliography

INTRODUCTORY

The best general introduction to the study of Swift's works is still found in:

Ricardo Quintana, *The Mind and Art of Jonathan Swift*, 1936; reprinted 1953 with additions to the notes and bibliography.
—— *Swift: an Introduction*, Oxford 1955, paperback 1962 is a briefer work.

TEXT

The standard collected editions of Swift's writing are:

Herbert Davis, ed., *Prose Works*, Shakespeare Head, Oxford, Fourteen volumes 1939–63; last volume with index still to come.
Sir Harold Williams, ed., *Poems*, Oxford, three volumes 1937; second edition 1958. The notes are indispensable. The single, unannotated volume of collected poems edited by Herbert Davis, Oxford 1967, is also excellent.
Sir Harold Williams, ed.; *Correspondence*, Oxford, five volumes 1963–5.

There are several useful editions of Gulliver's *Travels*, including those edited by:

Harold Williams, Everyman's Library, 1940.
Herbert Davis, *Prose Works of Swift*, volume XI, with an introduction by Harold Williams.
Louis A. Landa, Riverside edition (paperback), Cambridge, Mass. 1960. This has a useful introduction, notes and a list of biographical dates.
R. A. Greenberg, Norton paperback, New York 1961. This has excellent notes, bibliography and a selection of criticism.
P. Dixon and J. Chalker, Penguin English Library (paperback) 1967, with brief notes as well as a readable introduction by Michael Foot.

There are also independent editions of major and difficult works, as, for instance:

A. Guthkelch and D. Nichol Smith, *A Tale of a Tub* with *The Battle of the Books*, Oxford, second edition 1958.

BIOGRAPHY

The fascination of unravelling the complexities of Swift's life has invaded criticism of his works to an extent hardly equalled in English literature, so that biographical considerations and problems cannot be summarily excluded from the evaluation of his work in quite the happy way they often are.

H. Craik, *Life of Swift*, two volumes 1894, is still valuable for its facts.

I. Ehrenpreis, *Swift: The Man, His Works and the Age*, two volumes 1962–7; one more volume to come. This is an impressive large-scale work with a brilliant deployment of detail, and with some excellent critical remarks, but some arguable historical, social and 'psychological' interpretation.

——, *The Personality of Jonathan Swift*, 1958, is a shorter work giving a useful crisp treatment of some myths that have grown up around Swift.

Two biographical works which attempt a psychological profile of Swift are:

E. Hardy, *The Conjured Spirit*, 1949, which is unconvincing.

P. Greenacre, *Swift and Carroll: A Psychoanalytical Study of Two Lives*, New York 1955, which is orthodox Freudianism, but more amusing than valuable as criticism.

A shorter study on similar lines is:

N. O. Brown, 'The Excramental Vision' in his book, *Life against Death: The Psychological Meaning of History*, 1959; reprinted in Tuveson (see below). This may be less orthodox psychology, but makes a real attempt to deal with Swift's scatological writing, and to generalise some useful critical judgements. The essay deals partly with Gulliver's *Travels*.

CRITICISM

There are four useful general collections of essays on Swift's writing:

Herbert Davis, *Jonathan Swift: Essays on his Satire and Other Studies*, Oxford, paperback 1964, contains one essay specifically on Gulliver.

M. P. Foster, ed., *A Casebook on Gulliver among the Houyhnhnms*, New York, paperback 1961, contains the text of Book IV of the *Travels*, twenty-six pieces variously interpreting the voyage from Walter Scott to the present day, and an extensive bibliography.

A. N. Jeffares, ed., *Fair Liberty was All his Cry*, 1967, is a mixed bag, which, however, reprints useful essays by Kathleen Williams on Swift's imagery, F. R. Leavis on the irony of Swift (see below), and George Orwell, on Gulliver's *Travels*. It also includes an essay from a professional, medical point of view by T. G. Wilson on Swift's personality. Its most valuable features are Ricardo Quintana's evaluative article, 'A Modest Appraisal: Swift Scholarship and Criticism, 1945–65', and Claire Lamont's exhaustive 'Checklist of Critical and Biographical Writings on Jonathan Swift, 1945–65'.

E. Tuveson, ed., *Swift: a collection of critical essays*, Twentieth Century Views, paperback 1964. This contains a great deal on Gulliver's *Travels*, and a useful short bibliography.

From the vast amount of critical writing on Swift's works may be selected as especially worth while:

W. B. Ewald, *The Masks of Jonathan Swift*, Cambridge, Mass., and Oxford 1964, is the most solid discussion of Swift's use of *personae*, or masks.

F. R. Leavis, 'The Irony of Swift' in *The Common Pursuit*, 1952, Peregrine paperback, 1966.

M. Price, *Swift's Rhetorical Art: A Study in Structure and Meaning*, Yale Studies in English, Yale 1953.

K. Williams, *Jonathan Swift and the Age of Compromise*, Kansas, 1958. This discusses from an orthodox standpoint Swift's notions of reason.

From the writings on Gulliver's *Travels* may be selected:

A. E. Case, *Four Essays on Gulliver's Travels*, Princeton 1945.

C. H. Firth, 'The Political Significance of *Gulliver's Travels*', *Proceedings of the British Academy* IX, 1919.

S. H. Monk, 'The Pride of Lemuel Gulliver', *Sewannee Review*, Winter 1955; reprinted in Foster (see above).

Marjorie Nicolson and Nora Mohler, 'The Scientific Background of Swift's Voyage to Laputa', *Annals of Science* II, 1937; reprinted in Jeffares (see above), and also available in Nicolson, *Science and Imagination*, Cornell and Oxford, paper back 1956.

Index